SUCCESS IS YOURS, NO EXCUSES:
A Coach's Perspective

By
Jason Kent, B.S., M.S.S.,M.A.Ed.

Copyrights Notice

No part of this book can be transmitted or reproduced in any form including print, electronic, photocopying, scanning, mechanical, or recording without prior written permission from the author.

All information, ideas, and guidelines presented here are for educational purposes only. This book cannot be used to replace information provided with the device. All readers are encouraged to seek professional advice when needed.

While the author has taken utmost efforts to ensure the accuracy of the written content, all readers are advised to follow the information mentioned herein at their own risk. The author cannot be held responsible for any personal or commercial damage caused by misinterpretation of information or improper use of the information.

Published By: Books For Athletes
www.BooksForAthletes.com

Bibliography

For nearly 28 years, Coach Jason Kent has coached and trained student athletes at all levels of competition as a head coach and assistant men's basketball coach in the NCAA, NAIA, AAU basketball and boys' high school basketball. Coach Kent has had 20 of his former student athletes move on to play professional basketball.

Coach Kent specializes in recruitment, player development, mentoring, and strength & conditioning. By instilling hard work ethic, determination and discipline in his coaching and training technique, Coach Kent is known for his ability to maximize abilities and propel students to their full athletic potential.

Coach Kent is a Scout, Gold license USA Basketball Coach, he has partnered with the Jr. NBA, he is a Lead Clinician with Breakthrough Basketball, an SDC Scholarship Camp Director for Chicagoland area and National Evaluator and Training Consultant for World Basketball Exposure.

Coach Kent and his Wife Anna have two children Jayson (Indiana State University and Janae (LSU).

Dedication

I would like to thank my family for their continue support throughout the years as I have been on this journey. I would also like to thank all the players who I have trained, coaches who have mentored me, coaches and staff who have worked for me, players who have played for me and families who have trusted me with their scholar athletes.

I have been truly blessed and I would not have the experience and skills I have today if it was not for my Lord and Savior Jesus Christ.

Table of Contents

Bibliography 3
Dedication 4
Introduction 1
Self-Check 3

No Excuses For Not Training and Preparing 5
Chapter One: Excuses Athletes Use 7
"Need An Excuse To Validate Your Self" 7
"Society doesn't make it easy for women to succeed in sports" . 8
"Bad Games Happen" 9
"I'm In A Slump" 10
"My coaches don't know what they're doing" 11
"My teammates are slacking off" 11
"The trainer/coach is holding me back from being successful" 12
"The Environment is Tanking My Performance" 13

Chapter Two: No More Excuses! 15
Don't make excuses, make changes. 15
Everyone makes excuses. 16
Change your mindset and reset your habits." 16
Trust and believe in yourself. 17
Stop comparing yourself to others. 17
Take action and become self-disciplined. 17
The Importance of Hard Work – take out 18
Create a to-do list 18

    Delegate tasks and responsibilities 19

    Make time for your passion. 19

    Keep your eyes on the prize 19

    Surround yourself with positive, driven people......................... 19

Chapter Three: Overcoming Excuses Not To Train 21

Chapter Four: Seven Effective Ways, To Make Your Training Effective And Engaging 25

    1) Take initiative.. 25

    2) Begin with the end in mind 25

    3) Put first things first. 26

    4) Consider win-win scenarios 27

    5) Prioritize understanding over being misunderstood. 27

    6) Collaborate 27

    7) Make the saw sharp 28

Chapter Five: The Mental Game Is Real 31

Chapter Six: Bye To Excuses, Hello To Wisdom 35

Chapter Seven: The Final Straw... 37

The Champion Approach 39

Chapter Eight: The G.O.A.T. Michael Jordan 41

Chapter Nine: Everyone Can't Be Like Mike 43

Chapter Ten: Think like a Champion and Work Like an Athlete 47

Chapter Eleven: Create Your Own Opportunities 51

The Game Winner 55

Chapter Twelve: Coach Kent's Breakdown 57

    Be determined and set goals. 57

    Stay humble, stay hungry, and don't forget where you came from. 57

    Everything is a learning experience. 58

    Commit yourself to your craft. 58

Set up a workout routine and diet plan, monitor progress, and adjust as necessary. 59

Never, ever give up. 59

Coach Kent's Bonus For Parents 63

Chapter Thirteen: Knowledge Is Power 65

What is an elite athlete and what does it require? 66

References 81

Introduction

Do you feel like your life has been on autopilot lately? Do you feel like you're stuck in some sort of rut, going through the motion's day by day? Are you having trouble sticking to goals and habits that are important to you? Better yet, are you where you want to be in life? If not, then why not?

Life is full of potential reasons why people don't, won't, or can't, achieve their goals and dreams. They are called excuses, and we all have made them at some point. Making an excuse is an attempt to lessen the blame, justify, or defend why we fell short of an accomplishment. Finding reasons why we can't or won't do something is easy. On the other hand, setting achievable goals and sticking to the plan is the hard part.

Why do some people achieve their goals while others fail to accomplish the simplest of tasks? One's mental approach makes the difference. People who don't achieve their goals give up, make excuses, and settle for less than they want in life. Others reach their desired destination due to their grit, determination, and perseverance. Successful athletes like Jayson Kent, Darin Ames Jr. and Janae Kent epitomize these three qualities.

Action and accountability are necessary if you aspire to elevate from where you are today to where you want to be tomorrow. The difference between those who achieve their goals and those who do not is how often you make excuses and how quickly you change that behavior. The sooner you do this, the sooner you'll see results. It's time to stop making excuses. The following infographic will help you break this cycle so you can achieve your goals.

Self-Check

Our student athletes' chances of success are not being facilitated by society. You only see people seeking easy money and fame without making any sacrifices. What happened to putting in the necessary effort, being determined, setting goals, and then working tirelessly to make your dreams come true? When you consider our society as a whole, you will see that if something is not available to you right away or is not provided for you, you will give up and look for something else that will give you what you want without requiring you to put any effort into it.

Consider how sports have changed over time. Many athletes today are all about the quick and easy approach rather than the old school way of long hours and staying dedicated no matter how long it could take or hard it may be.

I was aware as a child that my mother couldn't afford to send me to college. Hell, she was already supporting me as best she could by working two jobs. So, in order for me to be successful, I prioritized my basketball aspirations over things that brought me no value. I did not want my mother to fret about my college situation.

Today's athletes have access to all the best facilities and gear, social media, AAU teams, shoe company teams, apps, and technology to monitor their development. When something doesn't go their way, athletes now tend to complain and place the blame elsewhere rather than on themselves. Making videos, having sex, playing video games, posting on social media, sleeping all day and all night, drinking, and smoking seem to have replaced honing one's craft as the top priority for athletes. It's not that athletes are lazy or amoral, it's that they're so focused on things that brings no value or makes a direct impact to their overall success. A number of athletes are overlooking their true priorities, and their careers because they feel they can make it up at another time or wait for someone to give them something or makes up excuses to why they are not having success!

No Excuses For Not Training and Preparing

Jason Kent, B.S., M.S.S., M.A.Ed.

Chapter One:
Excuses Athletes Use

"There Is Nothing More Detrimental To An Athlete Than Making Excuses"

In a sport that is predicated on the concept of failure, it's easy for players to begin making excuses at some point during their careers. When you're going through it, it's easy to start blaming your surroundings or teammates and not put the blame where it belongs: on yourself. It's also easy to make your coaches or teammates scapegoats when things aren't going your way. This happens in every sport and with every athlete, no matter how successful they become. When an athlete makes excuses, they are essentially saying, "I don't believe I am capable of performing because of these external factors." Letting go of any excuse and placing the blame on yourself is crucial for maximizing your potential as an athlete and getting out of that negative space you've been stuck in for so long.

Here are some things you should never say if you want to get out of a negative space and reach new heights as an athlete:

"Need An Excuse To Validate Your Self"

"I remember playing pick-up basketball in the summer of 1992 at Ohio University with my new college teammates. The games were extremely fast. Those guys jumped, ran, defended, and shot the ball at a high level. Being that I was a high school All American I wasn't worried initially. After two weeks, I realized that I could neither get

my shot off, drive to the basket, nor guard anyone. I made excuses in attempt to save face for not living up to the hype. Excuses justified my struggle, so I thought." Coach Kent

As an athlete you have a certain swag about yourself and confidence in your abilities when it comes to your particular sport and when your swag or confidence comes into question you create excuses to validate yourself to save face.

How many times have you gone to watch a basketball player who is considered to be the man/girl. You are expecting to see a show and that athlete knows you are there to watch him/her put on a show. The game starts and all of sudden you notice that athlete crying about getting fouled, not getting calls, the defender grabbing their jersey, someone not running the right play, or a teammate throwing a bad pass. Many basketball fans see athletes displaying their emotions in a negative way and making excuses because they were unable to have success or live up to their own hype. Making excuses to validate themselves is easier than fighting and pushing through the tough times. Unfortunately, we are seeing more and more athletes use excuses to validate their lack of performance.

As an athlete it's crucial to be strong mentally and to believe in your skill set. You must learn to control your emotions and put yourself in the best position to succeed.

"Society doesn't make it easy for women to succeed in sports"

"As part of the Education Amendments of 1972, Title IX prohibited gender-based discrimination in any school or any other education program that receives funding from the federal government. Even with this, women still face many challenges in sports today. For example, WNBA salaries are far from NBA salaries in the United States. Not to mention this includes traveling thousands of miles abroad just to be paid their worth."

Yes, society doesn't make it easy for women to succeed, but that doesn't mean you can use it as an excuse. You must be resilient in your pursuit of success and overcome any obstacle you are presented with. You must be ruthless in your pursuit of success and be willing to make sacrifices and take risks to get to where you want to be. Again, it is not as easy for women to succeed in sports as it is for men, but you can overcome that with hard work, perseverance, and a positive mindset. Anything is possible.

"Bad Games Happen"

"Coach Hunter, my head coach, put me in the game in the Mid-American Conference quarterfinals and I blew it. I missed an easy shot and allowed my man to score. Coach Hunter replaced me and told me to get my mind right.

He gave me another opportunity in the second half. I gave up a backdoor layup, missed a jump shot, and committed a personal foul. It seemed as if nothing I did went my way that game. I sat next to Mike Reese on the bench and told him that I was struggling. "No, you're not!" Mike said. "Just relax and play your game because we're going to need you."

The excuse I gave for my poor performance didn't have anything to do with basketball. Oddly enough, it took some encouragement from my teammate to help me see the bigger picture. I stopped making excuses and immediately bounced back. I returned to the game and scored 10 points to help my team beat Kent State University."

Bad games happen to every athlete. No matter how good you are or how much you believe in yourself, there will be moments when you fail, and fail miserably. Many players don't realize that until they are later down the road but those are the ones who have learned to put the blame on themselves, own up to it, and move on. Realizing that you have the power to overcome your mistakes and come back stronger is crucial to success. The next time you find yourself having a bad game and making excuses, remember that it's up to you to get out of that rut. You are the only one who can change your mindset and put yourself in the best position to succeed. You can do it, and you will do it.

"I'm In A Slump"

"The passing of my Aunt Shelia of HIV in 1992 messed my head up. I found myself in another slump in a few practices soon after, and I used her death as an excuse. David Grear, an assistant coach at the time, made it make sense. He explained that I wasn't in a slump and that my aunt's passing weighed on my mind and heart. There will be times when things aren't favorable on or off the court but locking in mentally will help you overcome the situation."

Statistically, you're going to go through slumps at some point in your career. It's inevitable, and sports are inherently unpredictable. The best teams and players lose games and have slumps just like everyone else. When you find yourself in a slump, it's important to identify why you're struggling. There could be a myriad of reasons why you're not playing to the best of your ability. You can't just blame it on a slump and excuse your way out of it. If you're playing poorly, it's time to take a good long look in the mirror and figure out what you're doing wrong. It's almost always something simple, like being out of shape, not practicing enough, or something similar to that. If you can't find a solution, work with a coach, trainer, or a teammate to find one.

"My coaches don't know what they're doing"

"There is a difference between basketball coaches and people coaching basketball.

Don't hesitate to make suggestions to your coach. Honestly, some coaches don't understand everything about the game. In many cases, underqualified parents fill in as coaches, especially in youth sports. Their expertise comes from watching games on television.

If you have an understanding of the game, played the game and you feel you can help the team or an individual get better, you should talk to the coach and offer the suggestions in a manner you are not telling them how to coach but rather offering a suggestion that could benefit the team or a certain individual."

It's easy to blame other people when you're not playing well. Coaches are easy targets when things aren't going your way, and it's completely natural. However, when you start making excuses like this, you're making a huge mistake. You may have a valid point in saying your coaches don't know what they're doing. If your coaches are rookies (or even if they have a few years under their belt), they may be struggling to figure things out. That doesn't make them bad coaches. If your coaches are making mistakes, you have to have the mental fortitude to push through and find how you and your team can be successful.

"My teammates are slacking off"

"This is a terrible excuse! Don't blame a teammate(s) for you having a poor performance. The best thing to do is offer a solution for helping your teammate(s) so your team can be successful and at the end of the day, one team, one goal."

Sometimes teammates can be the most frustrating people in the world. When you're going through a hard time and you want to develop a quick and easy excuse as to why you're not performing to the best of your abilities, it's easy to blame your teammates. When your teammates aren't performing to their abilities, it's difficult to shake off the feelings of inadequacy and disappointment. You're the one who has to go out on the court and perform, and when your teammates aren't helping you out, it can be really frustrating. However, when you begin making excuses like this, it only creates more animosity within your team. There is no point in blaming your teammates for slacking off; you're just creating an unnecessary distraction for everyone involved.

"The trainer/coach is holding me back from being successful"

"I followed a former high school basketball player who shot over 43% from mid-range. This guy could really shoot the pill. His efficient mid-range shot opened up the rest of his game. Consequently, he was benched and scolded for shooting the mid-range, while others were allowed to shoot it from anywhere.

The young man became discouraged because he couldn't utilize his mid-range skillset. Well, this particular individual refused to be held back. He continued to fight and eventually became a starter and major contributor with several big games."

This is a tricky one because it's not completely untrue. However, it is completely unproductive and it's just another excuse that will hold you back from being successful. If you aren't happy with the methods of your trainer and/or coach, it's okay to speak up. However, most of the time, when athletes blame the trainer and coach for their lack of success, it has nothing to do with their training. That's a dangerous road to go down. You have to be careful about how you approach your trainer and coach. You don't want to come across as disrespectful or ungrateful for the time and effort they put into helping you.

"The Environment is Tanking My Performance"

Lastly, an environment that fosters negativity or bad sportsmanship is not a good environment to be in. When you play in an environment like this, it's easy to begin blaming that environment for your struggles and not look at yourself. This is a huge mistake that will only make you feel worse about yourself. You need to be the leader of your team, the person who brings everyone up and out of the negativity. You need to be the person who does everything in their power to keep the team environment positive and focused on winning. The only way to do that is by taking care of yourself and looking at yourself critically. Remember this phrase. "YOUR VIBE ATTRACTS YOUR TRIBE!"

Jason Kent, B.S., M.S.S., M.A.Ed.

Chapter Two:
No More Excuses!

"As a coach the last thing you want are players and people around you who make excuses for their lack of performance every chance they get. This type of mindset doesn't' help or benefit anyone. You have to stand up and be accounted for and push pass any adversity that stands in your way. *Create the solutions to your excuses."*

Don't make excuses, make changes.

"When I became the head coach at Huston-Tillotson College, I came up with every excuse as to why I didn't think my players would be able to compete at a high level. The facilities weren't up to par enough at the time to draw a decent crowd. The players didn't even have their own locker room.

After my first week on the job, I reminded myself of why I wanted the job. This place had potential. The excuses I used didn't mean a hill of beans in the overall big picture. I humbled myself and developed relationships with the alumni and gathered other resources. With the help of countless others, we were able to get what we needed. It turned into an appearance in the Elite 8."

You have the power to shape your destiny. You can't change your past, but you can change what's happening in the present, and you can certainly change your future. Whatever your goals are, take the first step today. Break your larger goals down into smaller, more manageable steps. Focus on what you can do right now to move towards your goals.

Everyone makes excuses.

You don't have to look very far to find people making excuses. Everyone makes excuses. There isn't a person alive who has never made an excuse. We all have regrets from our past and worry about our future, but that doesn't mean we can't change our future. Some people make excuses for their behavior, and some make excuses for their circumstances. No matter what your reasons for not achieving success are, at the end of the day, they're all just excuses. The difference between successful people and people who make excuses is that successful people ignore their excuses while successful people use their excuses as fuel for their fire.

Change your mindset and reset your habits."

"I once coached a player who blamed me for his lack of playing time. He realized that he needed to hold himself accountable going into the next season. In turn, this player improved his strength, conditioning, and became a more of a student of the game. With the help of a trainer, he also improved his overall skill set. Overall, he grew tired of warming up the bench, so he put in the work to change his situation."

Most people who fail to achieve their goals don't do so because they lack the talent. Instead, they fail because they don't have the right mindset, or they don't have the right habits. Your approach and your habits have a huge impact on your success. If you're not making progress towards your goals, it's time to change the game. You must have the right mentality and believe in yourself so you can succeed and achieve your goals. Your habits will either help or hinder you as you work towards your goals. If you're not making progress towards your goals, then it's time to reset your habits. You need to identify the bad habits that are holding you back and replace them with good habits that will help you succeed.

Trust and believe in yourself.

"The word trust is defined as a firm belief in the reliability, truth, ability, or strength of someone or something. "J-Kent, You'll never write a book." So, I was told several years ago. I blocked them out and trusted myself."

It is okay if you are your number one fan. Have faith in yourself when no one else believes in you or supports you. Remember your life is yours and what you do with it is up to you. Shut out all of the people on the outside who are not supportive.

Stop comparing yourself to others.

Why are you comparing yourself to someone else? You have to be you and make the most of your opportunities and not try to live someone else's life because that is not going to help your dreams come to pass. So, if you are worrying about what others are doing, what achievements they are receiving, what attention they are receiving then your focus is off. Stop comparing yourself to others. Focus on what you can do right now to move towards your goals.

Take action and become self-disciplined.

Kobe Bryant was determined to be the best player to ever play the game. He worked his butt off and would get to the gym early and shoot two hours before the game just to focus his self. He did this every single game because he understood that hard work, determination, and sacrifice would take him to the highest level of success.

You have to be dedicated if you want to achieve your goals. You can't be a should have, could have, would have type of player. Remain disciplined, make your goals a priority and focus on accomplishing those goals on a daily basis. Don't ask for permission. Go out and take it!

The Importance of Hard Work – take out

Success is not given—it's earned. This is especially true when it comes to money and career success. No matter how intelligent, talented, or attractive you are, you can't expect to earn more if you aren't willing to put in the time and effort to earn it. In fact, most people who earn big money don't do it by accident—they're willing to put in the long hours and hard work necessary to succeed. If you want to earn more money, you're going to have to work for it. Earning a bigger salary requires a different formula than getting a promotion. You can't expect to achieve the same results while putting in the same amount of effort you've always used to get by. You have to push yourself and take on more responsibility in order to get to the next level. Willingness to put in the extra time and effort leads to promotion.

Not everyone is a natural when it comes to working hard. Some people are naturally driven and motivated to achieve great things, while others need help learning how to get motivated. If you're having trouble getting motivated and working hard, here are a few tips you can try:

Create a to-do list

Make a list of everything you have to do or want to do. This could include school-related tasks, game list, and career list. Once you've made your list, rank the items in order of importance. Try to add extra items that you want to achieve that don't have a deadline. This will help keep you motivated and on track.

Delegate tasks and responsibilities

"Teamwork makes a Dream work. One Team, One Goal"

Don't try to do everything yourself. Sure, it's good to have a can-do attitude, but you also don't want to burn yourself out. If you have a lot of tasks on your to-do list, try delegating a few of them to teammates or coaches. You could also outsource some of your less important tasks to trainers. This will allow you to focus your energy and attention on the things that really matter.

Make time for your passion.

If there's something you've always wanted to pursue, but it doesn't have a deadline, make time for it in your schedule. Sure, you may have a lot on your plate, but you can't achieve your goals if you don't make time for them. Wise people and successful entrepreneurs know how important it is to make time for your passion. Whether it's reading, writing, exercising, or something else, you have to carve out time for the things you love.

Keep your eyes on the prize

Whenever you find yourself getting distracted, you have to refocus your attention on your goals. Why did you set those goals in the first place? What are you trying to accomplish? Visualizing your goals and thinking about why they're important to you is a great way to stay focused and motivated.

Surround yourself with positive, driven people.

"Your vibe attracts your tribe."

You have to be careful who you choose to surround yourself with. You can't just pick any Joe Schmoe off the street and expect him to be your new best friend. You have to choose your friends wisely. Surround yourself with positive, driven people who are also working towards achieving their goals. This will help keep you motivated, inspired, and focused on your goals.

Chapter Three:
Overcoming Excuses Not To Train

Training, as we all know, is crucial to maintaining your skill set and taking your overall skill set to another level. But actually, doing it—well, that's a different story. We can always find excuses to skip or postpone our workouts, such as traffic, excessive work, scheduling conflicts, or fatigue. This prevents us from reaping the numerous benefits of becoming a better athlete.

Here are six of the most popular justifications for not training along with solutions.

1. *"I don't have time."* In today's hectic, overscheduled world, this is the most common excuse. Experts are curious as to how much time you set aside for other activities, like watching TV.

    Solutions: Utilize resistance bands or a treadmill while watching TV. You could use YouTube TV to watch a show without commercial interruption after working out, cutting an hour-long program down to 40 minutes.

    If your lack of exercise is due to your job, try to be more active there instead. Use the gym during lunch, use the stairs, avoid driving when walking is an option, and generally try to move more frequently.

2. *"I'm too exhausted."* This is another common excuse, and even

though it may not make sense, working out will give you more energy than before. That fatigue will vanish once you get moving, as if it never existed. That's because the endorphin release and increased circulation are both beneficial to your body. Try working out first thing in the morning to avoid having low energy levels as you start your day.

3. *"I don't have anyone to watch my brothers and sisters."* Experts advise bringing them along and exercising while they play.

   Additionally, make an effort to be active with your brothers and sisters.

4. *"If you allow it to be boring, it'll be boring."* Choose something you truly enjoy doing instead of something demanding or unpleasant. Everyone can find something; the challenge is finding it. For many people, working out with others is beneficial. To avoid getting bored, you can always switch up your workout routine.

5. *"I have a difficult time moving,"* The fact is that some people genuinely enjoy not being active. Try doing workouts in the water if your body hurts, and as you get stronger, your muscles will be better able to support your body and the pain will lessen. Athletic trainers can also assist people with more severe disabilities in engaging in safe, simple exercise.

6. *"You can combat this tendency to give up by setting small, doable goals that will allow you to experience some success."* You'll feel good if you train for 30 minutes a day for a week, and you might want to try 40 minutes a day the following week. To get support from people you know, it can also be helpful to keep a log of your activities and post them somewhere where you can see them. Logs also aid in getting you back on track by showing

you when you start to stray.

The American Surgeon General advises healthy adults to engage in 150 minutes or more of aerobic exercise each week. While this may seem like a lot, it only takes a little more than 20 minutes per day. Three ten-minute workouts are just as effective as a single twenty-to thirty-minute workout, and you may find it much easier to fit these shorter sessions into your busy schedule. So just think if you put this type of scheduling into your training.

In the end, those who don't find reasons not to work out prioritize their workouts. People always find time for the things they value, so they make time to train.

Jason Kent, B.S., M.S.S., M.A.Ed.

Chapter Four:
Seven Effective Ways, To Make Your Training Effective And Engaging

The foundation of effective discipline is the power of habit. When trying to maintain a fit and healthy body, discipline is crucial.

1) Take initiative

A big part of being proactive about your fitness is taking the initiative and responsibility to do the sport or physical activity of your choice. With or without other people's assistance.

Don't let solitude, isolation, or a lack of funds deter you from engaging in a sport, activity, or recreational activity if you want it badly enough. By seeking out information and experimenting with various basketball drills through practice, I was able to pick up a number of styles on my own.

You can just start if you have a sincere desire to learn and an open mind.

2) Begin with the end in mind

This is about having a goal that inspires you rather than just having a goal.

Therefore, focus your programs, exercises, workouts, and

training sessions on what you really want to accomplish with your body in order to achieve your own personal victory in fitness.

What do you want your body to be able to do?

What motivates you to aspire to embody those talents or abilities yourself?

What could you aim to achieve by learning or getting better at a particular sport, physical activity, or skill?

If you can develop the habit of visualizing exactly what you want from your training and why, you'll be naturally motivated to engage in any exercise, routine, or workout you decide to do.

3) Put first things first.

Training must be prioritized if it is to become a way of life. Therefore, you must either put training first in your heart or in your schedule if you want to make it a priority in your life.

Why do I say that? You will find a schedule that you can commit to consistently if your training is geared toward a workout session or exercise routine centered around a sport or physical activity that you are genuinely inspired and passionate about.

However, if your commitment to training is anything less than a burning passion and you find it difficult to show up, you should make it a priority in your schedule by working out first thing in the morning, first thing right after work, or, if possible, first thing when you get home. You'll have one less justification if you make it the first thing you do before doing anything else.

No matter what sport you play, a public victory is about developing habits that foster your development in a setting of group exercise. They are also the three behaviors that promote training interdependence. Interdependence can be a potent tool for leveraging collaboration to advance one's training while also serving as a source of leverage for the training of others.

4) Consider win-win scenarios

Whether you play for fun or compete, you're likely to have some humiliating experiences where you lose to a rival or simply feel less skilled than others.

When you think win-win, you can see the value in these humiliating situations because they are designed to make you more competitive by exposing your flaws.

Just take every setback as an opportunity to learn new things and ask new questions and receive new answers. You'd be surprised at how such humble experiences can make you aware of something you weren't before. Because you are unable to view yourself from a third-person perspective and because I am positive that you miss some details when writing in the first person, even criticism of your technique is valuable.

5) Prioritize understanding over being misunderstood.

Maintaining a student's mindset is very helpful in a group fitness setting. even if you happen to be the mentor, guide, coach, or teacher.

Each of us has a unique background and has engaged in various sports and activities that have given us different fitness-related experiences. Therefore, it's wise to be open and share knowledge about how to carry out particular exercises, skills, and techniques when working out in a group setting.

6) Collaborate

By using others to push and motivate you as well as to facilitate drills and routines that can yield exponential results that you would normally not be able to achieve on your own, group training has the additional benefit of compounding growth. Alternatively, not as quickly.

For instance, there are numerous tasks that call for collaboration. Towel sprints are a great example of combining exercises to increase your running's explosive power. One of many examples of using others for your own benefit is having someone hold you back by wrapping a towel around your waist as you drive out those legs to move forward.

The beauty of synergizing in training is that you can help others while benefiting yourself, so it doesn't end there. The towel sprint is an example of an exercise where you would need to take turns, but there are other exercises you can do with a group where everyone can benefit and none of you would benefit on your own.

7) Make the saw sharp

The practice of constantly practicing and perfecting your sport or physical activity is essentially sharpening the saw in terms of training. It's important to practice the fundamentals so that they gradually become more precise and help you become better at the sport or physical activity. In order to develop or improve a particular aspect of your training, it's also important to remain open to new information, drills, exercises, and routines.

Actually, there are only two key components to saw sharpening.

You are improving and honing the abilities you already possess that are essential for that sport or physical activity.

Learning, enhancing, and focusing on new abilities, talents, traits, and qualities that will help you become a better athlete in your sport or simply improve the standard or enjoyment of your physical activities.

It's very easy to get stuck in a static training routine and let yourself plateau, so the second point about sharpening the saw is very important. Having been there Ask yourself frequently if there are any training-related traits, qualities, or attributes that you want to hone, and then spend some time focusing your program laser-sharply on those. You could say that in order to respond to that question, you must apply habit 2 (start with the end in mind).

Habits are effective because, once formed, they reduce the need for strong willpower. These seven habits are expertly segmented.

You start out at the level of dependence, to put it another way. Whether that involves relying on a trainer or occasionally using raw willpower. When you achieve independence, which comes from mastering the three habits that will lead to your personal triumph, you will have developed the habits that will make incorporating training into your daily life effortless.

The three habits of your public victory can then be developed if you decide to join a group training environment from the level of independence. These behaviors will bring you to a state of interdependence where you can take advantage of the benefits of group collaboration to leverage rapid growth and progress in your training.

Jason Kent, B.S., M.S.S., M.A.Ed.

Chapter Five:
The Mental Game Is Real

Many sports call for both strong mental fortitude and physical prowess. Sports, in the opinion of the majority of coaches, are 90% mental and 10% physical. An extra edge can be very important, especially in sports where a tenth of an inch or a hundredths of a second can make the difference between a champion and a mediocre athlete. As a result, many athletes are using mental imagery to enhance their performance. Various applications of imagery in sports include problem-solving; improving confidence and positive thinking, reducing arousal and anxiety; reviewing and analyzing performance, preparing for competition, and keeping the mind sharp during injury (Porter & Foster, 1990). This section focuses on techniques for boosting self-esteem and maintaining motivation.

Strong Tools

The mind can be trained easily; all it takes is consistency, patience, and a little bit of daily time. Here are some popular methods for boosting self-assurance and developing mental toughness.

"The key is attitude." Poor attitude equals subpar work. Because of how closely our thoughts and our bodies are connected, our thoughts can affect how we feel, how we move, and how well we perform. You can't do something if you don't believe you can. That's how easy it is. Every day, try to think positively and to stop thinking

negatively. You can gradually hone your ability to see the world more firmly and optimistically. We all have the ability to get better at this skill with practice, even though for some people it might seem just as challenging as the physical preparation needed for their sport. All of us have heard of incredible human feats of strength that were made possible by the amazing power of positive thinking.

"Visualizations." On the track, in the court, and in your mind's eye, perfect practice leads to perfect performance. To hone your abilities with this strong tool, you must consistently practice it. You can continue your training program without becoming more exhausted by visualizing a perfect practice or skill. Studies have shown that during visualization, activity can take place in the nervous and musculoskeletal systems. Techniques like visualization are also excellent for unwinding and reducing anxiety before events. When injured athletes are unable to physically practice their skills or events, they can still benefit from the power of visualization.

"Mantras." Strong words and phrases that are frequently repeated in your mind can have a profound impact on attitude and performance. How would you feel if you constantly told yourself that you were weak, worn out, and pitiful? The inverse is also accurate. A visible, dynamic, and potent verbal and written mantra should be part of the event preparation process. Strong, powerful, smooth, fast, flowing, and other words are examples of mantras that may be effective for you. The most crucial step is picking a word or brief phrase that speaks to you. Repeating this phrase during your workouts and performances can help you perform better.

"Event planning." A good performance requires more than just rigorous physical preparation. No matter the finishing times or locations, you will always win the event in your head. Start putting your mental homework into practice.

"Eliminate Distractions." Tuning out distractions is the next step you must take to beat your rivals. Go somewhere quiet where

you can concentrate on what you need to do before a big game or race. Some athletes will play music that inspires them and makes them want to work hard. Do whatever feels right for you but make an effort to center both your body and your mind. The fewer distractions you have around you, the easier it will be to accomplish this.

"Utilize motivational tools." Finally, think about employing motivational tools to outsmart your rivals. This could involve reading your own personal goals and affirmations of self-worth again or simply watching videos of elite athletes performing for inspiration. Or perhaps you need to read motivational quotes to keep yourself focused and at your best by reminding you of certain things. Examine a few options to determine which ones work best for you. Even though some of these may seem silly, they can be very useful.

So be careful not to overlook the mental side of your game. It's crucial to your success, in fact.

Jason Kent, B.S., M.S.S., M.A.Ed.

Chapter Six:
Bye To Excuses, Hello To Wisdom

This research was put together after speaking with numerous elite athletes who are at the top of their sports. They all had advice for beginning athletes, despite the fact that their athletic and training demands were different.

1. *"Never assume that you will always have access to food."* Make sure you train as hard to perform as you eat to perform. There are numerous varieties of diets, each with a range of potential results. The secret is to consistently concentrate on your eating plan and avoid junk food and sweets.

2. *"Keep your word."* Regardless of how you are feeling, go and train if you say you will. You can always shorten the day but doing the work will make you mentally and physically stronger. Potential gains are killed by excuses.

3. *"Leave everything in the Gym."* When you leave the gym, you should be able to look in the mirror and respond with a resounding "YES." Outstanding athletes always push themselves. Train to beat previous bests and improve with each workout.

4. *"Defenses Create a Road to Nowhere."* By coming up with justification, you give yourself license to fail and feel okay about it. Be frank with yourself about your accomplishments.

Recognize that you are accountable for every choice you make.

5. *"Keep fighting when things go wrong."* Athletes encounter barriers, setbacks, obstacles, and injuries. However, this does not mean that the game is over. You can find ways to train until you are fully recovered, regardless of your current situation. Is there a broken arm? Work with the other arm while using one arm. Discover the mindset that will help you overcome.

6. *"Always defeat the person next to you."* Train as though you're going to compete. By striving to be the best in the room, you'll inspire others to match your level of commitment. In everything you do, go beyond the call of duty.

7. *"Set big goals and make every set and rep work toward that big goal without being afraid to fail."* Great athletes train to get stronger overall rather than just getting stronger in the short term. Make sure every exercise forces you to step outside of your comfort zone. Set goals; don't be afraid to try and fail; as long as you are making progress, you are a winner.

Chapter Seven:
The Final Straw

Nowadays, there is a lot of athletic pressure on athletes. They must juggle sports, school, family obligations, and other commitments, and there is pressure on them to "specialize" in one sport at a young age. The days when children could play one sport per season with little overlap are long gone. Most sports now have longer seasons, multi-season schedules, and many continue to play year-round. Travel teams are common, and there are many levels of competition. Even for the 12-and-under age group, many sports have additional conditioning drills. How do we, as parents, support our young athletes in this sometimes intense, fierce, and demanding world of youth sports?

We're keeping an eye on the prize! Not in terms of the final result, but rather in terms of the competition's objective. That is crucial. This process involves assessing the motivations of both you and your child. Consider your child's goals, the ones you have for them, and any that they may set for themselves as you consider the reasons why kids play sports. Goals range from boosting one's self-esteem, learning practical and life skills, exercising, and looking for college scholarships to having successful careers and realizing dreams. And it's crucial to know whose dreams they are.

In general, there are a lot of excellent reasons to encourage our kids to participate in sports. Sports participation fosters teamwork, life skills, a positive social influence, peer bonding, and a sense of belonging. While providing some kids with the space they need to work on task or skill mastery, physical exercise and skill development are also advantages. Some kids enjoy having fun, others enjoy competing, and still others enjoy both. A child's sense of confidence grows and blossoms while participating in a sport as a result of playing, participating, competing, belonging, and accomplishing. Sports should help a child's confidence grow rather than define it.

Where do the objectives of winning, excelling, specializing, and pursuing college scholarships (while still in elementary school) fit into these objectives? And how do they fit in without putting the child under undue stress, without running the risk of overuse injury, and without relying solely on winning or losing, statistics or records, to determine the child's self-confidence? What are the emotional benefits or costs? Parents must assess the goals: who set them, what do they offer the child, and at what cost or benefit? It's important to acknowledge the need for balance between the objectives and our children's full lives of family, school, play, activities, and sport. Parents should support their children's balance by acting with integrity and good sportsmanship.

Therefore, we can assist our athletes in working toward the most important goal—being content, healthy, confident, growing, and maturing young people—with honest assessment, balance, and parental leadership.

The Champion Approach

Jason Kent, B.S., M.S.S., M.A.Ed.

Chapter Eight:
The G.O.A.T. Michael Jordan

Michael Jordan is regarded as an American icon. Jordan was a key figure in basketball from the middle of the 1980s to the late 1990s, and he continues to be one of the most well-known athletes today. But the path his "airness" traveled was never simple.

Like everyone else, Michael Jordan has faced disappointment and rejection. Because he was deemed too short to play at the varsity level, Jordan's tryout for the high school basketball team was turned down. Jordan, however, did not give up on his aspirations. He joined the junior varsity team and played basketball there. Eventually, in his junior and senior years of high school, he advanced to another level.

Early in his life, Jordan demonstrated his perseverance in becoming the best basketball player he could be. The first thing Jordan taught us was how to bounce back from setbacks and rejection. Other college and professional games put his fortitude to the test, but he persisted until he was able to inscribe his name in the annals of athletic history.

In reality, Jordan's formula for success was a set of straightforward lessons that applied to life outside of sports as well.

- "*Accountability.*" Jordan accepted accountability for his deeds on and off the basketball court. One of his well-known quotations, "Some people just want to make things happen, others hope it happens, while the rest make it happen," makes this clear." Michael Jordan

- "*Taking chances.*" In addition to being regarded as the best basketball player, Jordan was well-known in a variety of other professions. He is also well-known for his work as an actor, businessman, and Olympian. If Jordan had not taken the risk and instead played in his comfort zone, he would not have achieved such greatness in this field.

- "Dedication and commitment." Jordan was a prime example of perseverance and training. Jordan would train hitting game winners so when it was time to win the game there was no pressure on him to hit the big shot because he trained for it already.

- *"Have fun playing."* People who are successful in their chosen professions do so because they enjoy what they do.

- *"Modesty."* Star athletes or players frequently lose sight of their humble beginnings and occasionally exhibit an air of arrogance.

- *"Setting goals."* Goals serve as a motivator for both adults and children, which is why it is crucial to set attainable or practicable objectives.

- *"Using the opportunity."* Jordan had faith in his ability to accomplish things. Opportunities should never be delayed; instead, they should be seized.

Amazingly, Jordan's experiences taught us valuable life lessons and skills that we frequently overlook or undervalue. Success for Michael Jordan wasn't really a secret; rather, it was a blend of tenacity, diligence, and passion.

Jordan, of course, has abilities we may never have. We might never be able to move at that same speed or with that same vertical leap, but when we do something, we are skilled at, passionate about, or that we love, we can undoubtedly come in second.

Chapter Nine:
Everyone Can't Be Like Mike

When watching a football, basketball, or softball game, someone might be impressed by an athletic play or support a certain team. In the end, they would realize that the goal was to triumph in the contest. It is only a game, win or lose. Athletics is much more than just a game, even though winning is the ultimate goal that all athletes strive to achieve. Future A-player employees can develop in athletics, especially at the collegiate level. An A-player is a high-ranking employee who excels as a leader and as a role model. One A-player can drastically alter a company, and with the right retention strategies, A-players will draw in more top talent.

The percentage of athletes who continue their athletic careers professionally is extremely low, according to the National Collegiate Athletic Association (NCAA), one in six NCAA football players will play in the NFL, one in ten women's basketball players will play in the WNBA, and one in four men's soccer players will play professionally after their college careers. 472,625 athletes nationwide competed in 23 NCAA sports during the 2013–2014 academic year. Unfortunately, the chances of playing professionally are very slim, so many gifted athletes must leave athletics after their college careers and go into the workforce.

The good news is that athletes are brought up to be excellent employees, which is great for many businesses. For the following reasons, I feel a businessman should take on an athlete as his next employee.

1. Athletes are goal oriented.
2. Athletes have resiliency.
3. Athletes are excellent communicators.
4. Athletes value teamwork.
5. Sportspeople are excellent time managers.

The majority of athletes have a strong desire to compete. Athletes compete not only against one another, but also with other teammates for a spot on the team. Each athlete has an obligation to perform because collegiate athletics is a business and their playing time and/or spot on the team could be in danger. Achievement-oriented people typically never feel satisfied and refuse to be complacent. It's critical to give athletes new objectives to work toward on a regular basis. They enjoy competing, and a company will gain a lot from an athlete's competitiveness.

Sports encourage perseverance and overcoming challenges in order to succeed. Athletes face a variety of challenges throughout their careers. It is expected of athletes to deal with injuries, adapt to uncontrollable situations like an umpire's strike zone, and compete all the way through a game, even when it seems like victory is out of reach. Greatness is achieved by the strong. For instance, in the 2004 American League Championship Series, the Boston Red Sox were trailing the Yankees by three games. It would have been easy to give up, but the Boston Red Sox didn't, and the baseball team displayed it's tenacity by winning four straight games before going on to win the World Series. Athletes fight, scratch, and claw to achieve their objectives; they won't let the uncontrollable defeat them. A worker who adopts this mindset will have a significant impact on the company and help to foster a successful culture.

An athlete must be well-versed in communication, especially in team sports. On the field, it is their responsibility to coordinate with teammates to carry out plays and inspire positive behavior through encouraging cheers and fostering a sense of teamwork. Any information that is exchanged between individuals constitutes communication, which is not just limited to verbal messages. Successful athletes are coachable and maintain constant communication with their teammates and coaches. Coachability is essential because, without buy-in from the coaching staff and teammates, communication breaks down, leading to a lack of confidence, trust, and indecision. As a manager, you want your team members to fully believe in the process, be receptive to constructive criticism, and express themselves through their actions, feedback, and willingness to be coached. An athlete will work for the success of the business because they are goal-oriented and competitive, which puts them ahead of non-athletes.

The greatest skill an athlete can bring to the workplace is probably the advantage of working as a team. Being team-oriented promotes altruism, respect for others' cultures and emotions, and serves as a symbol of something much greater than one person. Sportspeople are good team players who are aware of how their actions affect the team and organization. There will always be disagreements in a group, but when you spend more time with the same people than in your family, you develop interpersonal skills as you work toward a common objective.

Last but not least, a college athlete would be a valuable asset to a company because they have experience using their time effectively. All athletes must enroll in at least 12 credits and maintain a 2.0 grade point average in order to compete in the NCAA. Additionally, in order to compete in their sport, athletes must have a certain percentage of their degree completed each year. An athlete is also expected to perform well in a strength and conditioning program in addition to attending practice, depending on the division (I, II, or III) and the university. Most freshmen find it difficult to balance their first year of school, practice, and strength and conditioning, but by the end of their athletic careers, they have mastered time management. Having good time management skills helps people stay calm, avoid feeling overwhelmed, and perform better overall.

To sum up, a former student-athlete is a great choice for the position of a company's next A-player. College athletes have an impact both on and off the field, though it might not appear that way while they are competing in their sport. Athletics develops character and pushes participants beyond their perceived limits. Athletes always have a choice, and those who stick with it for a demanding but fulfilling four-year career develop into better people and athletes and gain the skills necessary to be useful members of society.

Chapter Ten:
Think like a Champion and Work Like an Athlete

Why do we find athletes so fascinating?

We consider the qualities and work ethic that athletes possess. Here are 6 very important qualities that all athletes can use for leadership and innovation:

1. *"Athletes are focused on their objectives."* They are aware that efficiency is enhanced by effectiveness. They put in more effort because they are aware that failure is merely a necessary condition for success.

2. *"They think like businesspeople."* They have a larger perspective and employ strategic thinking to put their goals into practice. They transform immediate objectives into long-term goals.

3. *"Athletes never give up, deal with the unavoidable, and are relentless."* Even if they lose their game, they fight until the very end. If they fail, they analyze the video to see what went wrong and look for wholesome approaches to approach the challenge again both physically and strategically. They exert a lot of effort to overcome their individual and collective challenges.

4. *"A lot of world-class athletes take a special approach to their sport."* They have created a unique style of playing the game based on their unique skill sets. Serena Williams, for instance, uses a distinctive two-handed backhand grip that differs from the standard backhand stroke used in tennis. Her aggressive baseline playing style is a deadly tool in her fight to outsmart her opponent and prevail.

5. *"Athletes are aware of the importance of leading a healthy lifestyle for their performance."* For optimum functionality, a healthy diet, regular exercise, and enough sleep are essential. The consequences are too severe without maintaining a balance in nutrition, fitness, energy, sleep, and general good mental and physical health.

6. *"Athletes comprehend the value of "team play."* They are aware of the reliance each team member has on the others. They make use of their advantages and strengthen their weaknesses. Team members receive training to support one another. The top tier of the organization, as well as the bottom tier, are all impacted by their contribution to the overall success of the organization. It is not only self-defeating but also detrimental to the team if they only think about "self" and become caught up in their ego.

Organizations, whether for-profit or nonprofit, seek out leaders with a champion work ethic who will act as supporters and motivators. Businesses are aware that overcoming challenges is essential for success. Training, attitude, dedication, respect, general fitness, teamwork, and a desire to develop are all necessary for success. These athletic qualities are essential for champion thinking. 1

---

[1] Source: Covey, Stephen R. The 7 Habits of Highly Effective People: Powerful Lessons In Personal Change. New York: Free Press, 2004. Print.

Critical Competencies for Good Athletes

There are a few reasons why I put "regarding" in quotation marks, including the fact that some people inherit the genetic makeup of their entire family and the extent to which parents and guardians encourage their children to be active and participate in sports. All I'm saying is that young children who inherit the genetic make-up of their professional sports-playing parents have an advantage over those whose parents never took an interest in the game.

Determination/Focus:

Without focus and determination, NO ONE, I repeat, NO ONE, can become a good athlete. If you don't, you'll slack off and lose interest in your goals. In my opinion, "determination" also refers to drive. Being more driven to excel as an athlete or in any other endeavor can give you an advantage over those who are attempting to surpass you. I believe that having the willpower or the drive to succeed at all costs is the definition of determination. Focus. Can you concentrate? Being focused on improving your athletic abilities is crucial because getting sidetracked can take you in the complete opposite direction. These include, in particular, soda, fatty foods, procrastination, and drugs. You will have a greater competitive advantage if you remain focused.

Strength:

I grant that some sports require less strength and conditioning than others, but why not strive to outperform the opposition in every way? In a small way, conditioning can translate into strength because, as you condition your body, it gets stronger. Being physically fit is necessary to become an athlete. A person must incorporate strength and conditioning exercises into their daily routine if they hope to compete in some kind of competition or earn a spot on a sports team.

Eye-Hand Coordination:

Simply put, coordination is a very difficult and important skill to have because without it, becoming an athlete will be much more challenging. Coordination is essentially the ability to react or respond quickly to an oncoming force. For lack of better terminology, coordination is very challenging. When a person's hands and eyes can work together to find the correct spot simultaneously, they have good hand-eye coordination

Chapter Eleven:
Create Your Own Opportunities

Are you genuinely committed to raising your performance, and are you prepared to go above and beyond? Or do you genuinely care but only opt to do what is convenient?

There is no right or wrong answer to this question; it is not a trick question. Be brutally honest and truthful with yourself, regardless of your response. Athletes frequently claim to be committed, but their behavior often says otherwise. Have you ever seen an athlete make excuses despite claiming to be committed? That person is not being honest with themselves as an athlete.

We are all familiar with the defensive line in sports. The tone is set by their posture. A strong defense should also have the ability to attack, pursue, and escape.

What if a sportsperson consistently behaves in this manner? He constantly takes a stand for his own cause, is prepared to strike out, looks for fault in others, defends his position, and abdicates responsibility by offering justification. It's exhausting to be on guard all the time like that.

Here are seven quick steps to make everything better.

1. *"Quit blaming other people no matter what has happened."* Start accepting accountability for your own actions. Examine the role that your mindset plays in your performance.

2. *"If there is a quality about another person that you don't*

like, it usually reflects a similar quality that you have that you don't like about yourself." By taking a look in the mirror, you can decide whether or not you want to change it.

3. *"Learn how to take action and modify your behavior."* Is shifting your attention, doing strength training, or taking better care of yourself and your diet the answer? Choose one or two new behaviors you can start practicing increasing your commitment.

4. *"Focus on your weaknesses rather than the strengths."* When I go out to evaluate players the one thing, I look at first is their weakest hand. I tell them you can tell a lot about a player by looking at how much time they put into their weakest hand because it translates in the game. "Your game is as good as your weakest hand." Lock in on your skill set don't allow your weakness to be a weakness.

5. *"Be open to stepping outside of the box and to different viewpoints."* Your next opportunity could be anywhere, at any time.

6. *"A game-changer is believing that you are a winner."* Your actions are affected by your perception. You channel the energy you previously used to resist stepping outside of your comfort zone.

7. *"You start to recognize challenges instead of obstacles."* The resistance is eliminated by shifting the focus. As you start walking toward your objective, your energy soars.

The altered viewpoint fosters a no-excuses attitude, which supports your ascent in the rankings. Things you had previously avoided become the next challenge for you to overcome. Being committed and being interested are opposite in polarity. Your dedication gives you the power to take whatever action is necessary. Explanations evaporate.

SUCCESS IS YOURS, NO EXCUSES: A Coach's Perspective

Many athletes, coaches, and consultants in the sports industry think that adding something leads to commitment. That impression is untrue. You were only interested enough to hold you back from inspired action. By removing distractions and obstacles, you can gain access to the energy required to focus on your goals.

A paradigm shift occurs when you decide to take the steps required to achieve your goal. The challenges that had kept you from acting are suddenly no longer challenges. They are merely the next obstacle you must overcome as you advance toward your objective.

Review the seven steps for enhancing personal accountability. Select one or two actions that you can start taking right away. There will be times when you revert to previous habits of thought or behavior. Refocus on the new decisions you are making now after you catch yourself doing that. Inner game strategies require practice, just like altering your technique does. What was once novel will eventually become comfortable and familiar.[2]

---

[2] Source: (Arzino, Caplan, & Goold, 1991) (J, Cotton, Kays, & Slaven) (Haddock, Christopher K; Poston, Walker S C; Heinrich, Katie M; Jahnke, Sara A; Jitnarin, Nattinee, 2016) (Jones, Stoler, & Suyama, 2013) (Babushkin, 2015) (Vysochina, 2017)

Jason Kent, B.S., M.S.S., M.A.Ed.

The Game Winner

Jason Kent, B.S., M.S.S., M.A.Ed.

Chapter Twelve:
Coach Kent's Breakdown

Be determined and set goals.

As a child, when I wanted something, I did whatever I could to get it. I didn't have a lot of money or fancy gear, but I made do with what I had and still reached my goals. There are times in life when you are not going to succeed No matter what you do, you will fail. It's important when you fail to understand why you failed so that you can adjust your approach and try again. You may fail at something five or ten times before you succeed, but it's important to keep trying. Failure is a step toward success, so you want to keep taking steps forward. What are your goals? What do you want to achieve? Whether it's graduating from college, starting a business, learning how to play an instrument, or being the best athlete you can be, you must be determined in order to succeed.

Stay humble, stay hungry, and don't forget where you came from.

As a child, I was always hungry, but it wasn't because I didn't have enough to eat. I was hungry for success, hungry for knowledge, and hungry to be the best that I could be. There will come a time in your life when you reach a high point. It might be in your career, as an athlete, or in some other area of your life. While you should be proud of what you have accomplished, you also need to stay hungry and humble. Before you reached that high point, you were hungry and determined to succeed. You worked hard and sacrificed a lot in order to reach your current point. Once you achieve success, it's easy to get satisfied, forget where you came from, and rest on your laurels. When you reach your goals, you have to stay hungry. You have to stay hungry to keep improving, to keep learning, and to keep growing. If you are successful, you have to remember that there are plenty of other people who want to be successful, too. You have to stay hungry and humble so that you can maintain that success.

Everything is a learning experience.

As an athlete, you should learn from every experience. Every game, every practice, every training session, every film session, and every mistake you make in life can teach you something. Think about the last game you lost. What caused you to lose? What mistakes did your teammates make? What could you have done better? Think about the last time you injured yourself or your knee, shoulder, or back hurt. What caused the injury? How could you prevent it in the future? Think about your last practice. What could you do better? What can you learn from the coach or your teammates? How could you be a better teammate? Everything that happens in your life can help you improve and achieve your goals. When you are young, you often have a lot of excuses for why you did something wrong or why you failed to do something right. You make excuses because you're young, you don't know any better, or you just don't want to put in the effort needed to succeed.

Commit yourself to your craft.

An athlete's craft is important for success. It's what you do best, and it's how you make a living. When it comes to your craft, you want to be the best at what you do. You want to make a name for yourself and be recognized for your greatness. If you're a basketball player, you want to be the best shooter on your team, the best scorer, and the best defender. You want to be so good that your coaches can't take you off the floor because you're always doing something special. If you're a musician, you want to be the best at what you do. You want to inspire people and make them feel something when they listen to your music. You want to be a leader and make others want to follow you. You want to push the boundaries of what is possible in your craft.

Set up a workout routine and diet plan, monitor progress, and adjust as necessary.

When you commit yourself to being great at your sport, you have to make sacrifices. You can't sleep all day and stay up all night. You can't eat junk food and drink alcohol every day. You have to be disciplined, do what's right for your body, and make sacrifices in order to succeed. One of the most important things an athlete can do is develop a workout routine. You need to know what exercises to do and how to do them so that you can build strength, speed, and agility. When you develop a workout routine, you also need to develop a diet plan. The right diet will give you energy, help you recover from your workouts, and allow you to build muscle when working out. Although it can be difficult to change your eating habits and workout routine, it's an important part of becoming the best athlete you can be.

Never, ever give up.

It's easy to get down on yourself when you feel like you're stuck in a rut. You're going to feel like you're never going to get out of it. You're going to feel like you're not good enough to do what you dream of doing. That's normal. Everyone goes through that at some point in their life. It's a normal reaction in a high-pressure environment like athletics. When you find yourself in a rut, make sure you keep these things in mind. Don't make excuses and let that negativity seep into your mental state. You must stay positive and optimistic if you want to get out of the rut and reach new heights as an athlete.

When you're young, you want to be successful, but you don't know what it takes to get there. You want to be rich, famous, and have lots of friends, but many of your goals aren't realistic. You must work hard and make sacrifices to achieve success. You can't drink alcohol, party all the time, and expect to excel in sports or in life. You want to be successful, but you have to put in the effort, make the sacrifices, and commit yourself to your craft. If you want to be successful, you have to make a decision to do something better with your life. You have to be decisive, focused, and dedicated. The key is to not let your emotions, or the emotions of others affect you. You have to make a decision and stick to it. You have to make sure that you're not being influenced by peer pressure or other outside factors that could cause you to make bad decisions. You have to be strong, confident, and committed to making the changes in your life that you know are necessary to achieve success.

When you're in a slump, it's easy to begin blaming anything and everything except for yourself. You have to ask yourself, "What can I do better?" and "What have I done to cause myself to play poorly?" instead of making excuses. When you are critical of your own performance and how you are going about your daily routine, you will be able to perform better and get out of your slump.

Successfully achieving your goals requires more than just wishing for it and hoping for the best. It requires putting in the effort and taking action. If you're having trouble getting motivated and working hard, try implementing some of these tips. There are two sides to every story, and these are the facts behind what goes into making excuses and achieving goals.

At the end of the day, reaching your goals requires taking action.

This means that you must stop making excuses and start making changes. You consider changing your mindset and reset your habits. You have to trust and believe in yourself. You have to stop comparing yourself to others. You have to take action and become self-disciplined. You have one life to live and one chance to make it great. You have to live your life and you have to make the most of your opportunities. You have to achieve your goals and make the most of your life. Reaching your goals starts with taking action, especially when you don't feel like it. Discipline and perseverance are two qualities that are inherent in athletes, and they will take you far. Athletes make decisions based on what is best for them and their future, not based on what other people may think. It's time to put excuses aside and reach for the success!

Jason Kent, B.S., M.S.S., M.A.Ed.

Coach Kent's Bonus For Parents

Jason Kent, B.S., M.S.S., M.A.Ed.

Chapter Thirteen: Knowledge Is Power

The task of controlling the emotions that game competition brings is extremely difficult for parents who get involved and support their athletes. Youth athletes' levels of confidence can easily be impacted competition. Youth athletes without a doubt require support during sporting events because there are many emotional ups and downs. Your ability to support your child's will increase with how involved you are as a parent. The main thing that parents should keep in mind is that getting too involved can impede their child's development as an athlete. There's a thin line there that needs to be acknowledged and never crossed. It is the parent's responsibility to keep that boundary.

Parents of young athletes should undoubtedly assist their offspring with self-confidence, physical skill development, and the integration of life lessons into game experiences and challenges. The key here is to be aware of your child's level of enjoyment and to make sure they are having fun despite any difficulties.

Children, the team, and the coach can all benefit greatly from parents who can assist their young athletes in honing their physical and mental abilities during practice and competitive games. Youth athletes who participate in competitive sports and their supportive parents undoubtedly gain some wonderful experiences and memories. The team benefits the most from the supportive and friendly parents.

Parents who volunteer to instruct or coach their kids or other team members are accepting more responsibility. That accountability entails risk. Parents who are qualified to coach or train in that particular sport must coordinate their lessons with the methods and objectives of the coach. Parents who believe they are smarter or more knowledgeable than the coach put the team at risk.

When parents become overly emotionally invested in their child's improvements and setbacks, this poses another risk that could harm young athletes. You can anticipate issues after this occurs. When overly involved parents cross the line and start acting more like controllers than helpers, issues start to arise between the parent and child.

The relationship between parents and young athletes can deteriorate to the point where the child no longer finds enjoyment in the sport when a parent adopts a controlling attitude. He or she stops enjoying the game experience, plays poorly, demoralizes the team, and starts to dislike their parents. Everyone who is involved loses when egos take over.

Parents of young athletes should be supportive but not too involved. The wise parent is the one who is aware that their child will come to their own conclusions in due course.

What is an elite athlete and what does it require?

It will take effort to develop into any kind of true athlete. Nothing, but nothing, can replace perseverance and hard work. Success is attainable with the right combination of mental and physical preparation. The majority of athletes are unaware of what it takes to be a true athlete. The majority of athletes believe that just because they spend an hour or two working out in the gym, a halo appears over their heads.

Real athletes go above and beyond what other athletes won't.

Some athletes have intrinsic motivations that cannot be coached. They are driven by an internal drive for excellence that no coach on earth can teach them how to cultivate. You will have a champion on your hands if the athlete is self-driven and has a "drive" for success. It's time to consider switching sports if you have to constantly remind your young athlete to practice or play. Either they possess "it" from the inside out or they don't. It's okay if they don't have it. Just be aware that your chances of reaching the top of the sport are less likely.

The Five Steps of Keeping 100

1. *"knowledge and comprehension."* Regarding your athlete's athletic ability, be realistic. It's not a given that a person can advance to the next level even if they perform well at a given level. If your young athlete is truly elite, there are obvious signs that will indicate this. Learn as much as you can about the sport that your athlete is interested in.

2. *"How to cooperate, not compete, with the athlete."* Your children come first, not you. Don't let your kids live your lives for you. It's time to give them their chance since you already had your chance when you participated. Help them, don't follow them around.

3. "Even if your athlete is above average or elite, realize that there is still much work to be done." Each level an athlete strives for will get harder and harder. Keep them diligently working, mentally focused, and modest.

4. *"In order to fully comprehend this, you must first acknowledge the practicalities of sports."* There is a young person working incredibly hard right now to improve themselves. Just be aware that some young people will stop at nothing to succeed. There is a way to improve your athletic abilities, whether you are an average or elite athlete. There is no such thing as a bad athlete,

in my opinion. But if you don't have the drive or passion to improve, you might want to set other objectives.

5. *"If your athlete is only average [or even below average] at their sport, accept it."* That's alright; not everyone can be like Mike. It doesn't preclude them from making an effort to advance to the next level.

Being a top athlete requires a combination of passion, self-discipline, and the capacity to endure discomfort and stress while still having fun. It's not just talent because, one day, your athlete will look around and see talent that is either equal to or greater than their own.

Coach Kent & Janae Kent

Coach Kent & Jayson Kent

SUCCESS IS YOURS, NO EXCUSES: A Coach's Perspective

Coach Kent, Anna Kent & Darin "Dai Dai" Ames
(trained with NextLEVEL 24)

Coach Kent, Anna Kent & Michael Collins
(Former College Player of Coach Kent)

SUCCESS IS YOURS, NO EXCUSES: A Coach's Perspective

Coach Kent & Janae Kent (2023 Signee LSU)

Jayson Kent (Player at Indiana State University)

Coach Kent's NextLEVEL 24 Pro AM Team

Coach Kent, Anna Kent & Cameron Grear
(trained with NextLEVEL 24 / Assistant College Coach 2023)

Jayson Kent (Player at Indiana State University)

Coach Kent & Molly Franson (trained with NextLEVEL 24)

Janae Kent High School Senior Night

SUCCESS IS YOURS, NO EXCUSES: *A Coach's Perspective*

Jayson & Janae Kent

Coach Kent's Huston - Tillotson University Players and Staff 2001 - 2002 Elite 8 team. (Not all members pictured)

Coach Kent & Huston- Tillotson University Staff in the 2001-2002 Elite 8

SUCCESS IS YOURS, NO EXCUSES: A Coach's Perspective

Coach Kent & Brother Jordan Fair

Coach Kent, Anna Kent & Brother Anthony Kent

References

Arzino, P., Caplan, C., & Goold, R. (1991). *Physical fitness training*. Hayward, CA (United States): International Nuclear Information System.

Babushkin, B. Y. (2015). Psychological support of pre-season training of highly skilled athletes. *researchgate*.

Haddock, Christopher K; Poston, Walker S C; Heinrich, Katie M; Jahnke, Sara A; Jitnarin, Nattinee. (2016). The Benefits of High-Intensity Functional Training Fitness. *SEALFIT*.

J, R., Cotton, R. A., Kays, A. C., & Slaven, E. J. (n.d.). *Shoulder Injuries in Individuals Who Participate in CrossFit Training*. CrossFit.

Jones, D., Stoler, G., & Suyama, J. (2013). Effectiveness of three just-in-time training modalities for N-95 mask fit testing. *worldwidescience*.

London RA, C. S. (2011). A longitudinal examination of the link between youth physical fitness and academic achievement. *Journal of School Health*, 400–408.

Covey, Stephen R. The 7 Habits of Highly Effective People: Powerful Lessons In Personal Change. New York: Free Press, 2004. Print.

Mechanic D, H. S. (1987;28). Adolescent competence, psychological well-being, and self-assessed physical health. *Journal of Health and Social Behavior*, 364–374.

Miller KE, M. M. (2005). Untangling the links among the athletic involvement, gender, race, and adolescent academic outcomes. *Sociology of Sport*, 178–193.

Monti JM, H. C. (2012;22). Aerobic fitness enhances relational memory in preadolescent children: The FITKids randomized control trial. *Hippocampus*, 1876–1882.

Okhlopkov, I. C. (2015). *Methodological support of training.*

Vysochina, N. (2017). Goal-setting in sport and the algorithm of its realization.

Made in the USA
Middletown, DE
10 May 2024

53976793R00051